SKILL BUILDERS
FOR
ALTO SAXOPHONE

COMPILED AND ARRANGED BY
STUART ISACOFF

Educational Consultant: Bob Santin

ED 3206
ISBN 978-0-634-00041-6

G. SCHIRMER, Inc.

DISTRIBUTED BY

HAL•LEONARD®
CORPORATION
7777 W. BLUEMOUND RD. P.O. BOX 13819 MILWAUKEE, WI 53213

CONTENTS

SKILL BUILDERS
for E♭ Alto Saxophone

Compiled and Arranged by
Stuart Isacoff

FOLK-ROCK AND FOLK FUN

Scarborough Fair

Old English

48144c

House of the Rising Sun

5

American Folksong

Moscow Nights

Russian Folk Song

Amazing Grace

Gospel Song

48144

Morning Has Broken

Gaelic Hymn

Man of Constant Sorrow

American Folksong

Greensleeves

Old English

Hey Ho, Anybody Home?

American Folk Round

Kum Ba Ya

African Folksong

Childgrove

English Folksong

Blaw the Wind Southerly

English Folksong

Simple Gifts

Shaker Hymn

La Bamba

Spanish Folksong

The Ash Grove

English Folksong

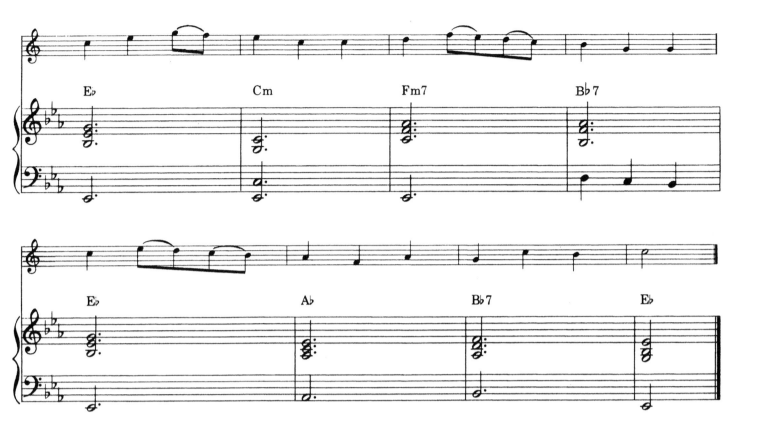

Go Tell Aunt Rhody

American Folksong

Skip to My Lou

American Folksong

Crawdad

American Folksong

Old Joe Clarke

Traditional Fiddle Tune

Little Maggie

Traditional Fiddle Tune

The Rakes of Mallow

Traditional Fiddle Tune

Will the Circle Be Unbroken

American Folksong

26

48144

Cripple Creek

Traditional Fiddle Tune

28

48144

Arkansas Traveller

Traditional Fiddle Tune

Soldier's Joy

Traditional Fiddle Tune

John Henry

American Folksong

Turkey in the Straw

Traditional Fiddle Tune

Worried Man Blues

Traditional Blues

Crossroads

Country Blues

Frankie and Johnny

Traditional Blues

Rock My Soul

Spiritual

Let My People Go

Spiritual

Joshua Fought the Battle of Jericho

Spiritual

St. James Infirmary

Jo Primrose

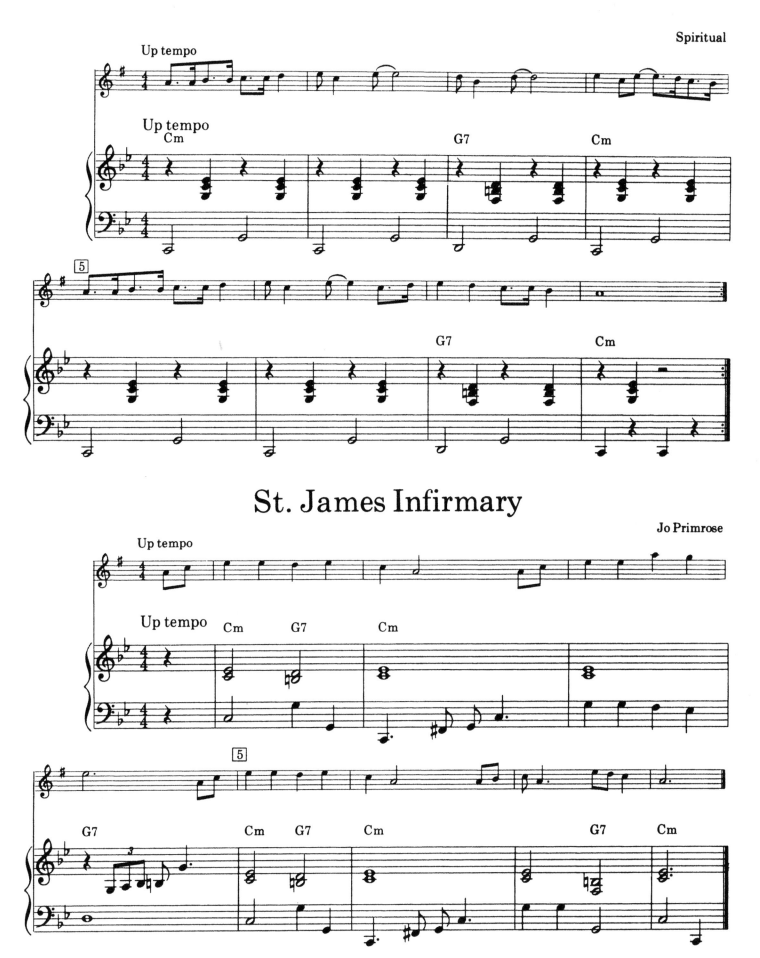

Mama Don't 'low

Folk Blues

Candyman

Country Blues

Camptown Races

Stephen Foster

Shortnin' Bread

Folk Blues

The Entertainer

Scott Joplin

Swing Low, Sweet Chariot

Spiritual

Pistol Blues

Bo'Weevil Jackson

The Chrysanthemum

Scott Joplin

SKILL BUILDERS
FOR
ALTO SAXOPHONE

COMPILED AND ARRANGED BY
STUART ISACOFF

Educational Consultant: Bob Santin

G. SCHIRMER, Inc.

DISTRIBUTED BY

HAL•LEONARD®
CORPORATION
7777 W. BLUEMOUND RD. P.O. BOX 13819 MILWAUKEE, WI 53213

CONTENTS

SKILL BUILDERS

for E♭ Alto Saxophone

Compiled and Arranged by
Stuart Isacoff

FOLK-ROCK AND FOLK FUN

Scarborough Fair

Old English

House of the Rising Sun

American Folksong

48144c

Eb Alto Saxophone

Moscow Nights

Russian Folk Song

Amazing Grace

Gospel Song

Morning Has Broken

Gaelic Hymn

Man of Constant Sorrow

American Folksong

E♭ Alto Saxophone

Greensleeves

Old English

E♭ Alto Saxophone

Hey Ho, Anybody Home?

American Folk Round

Kum Ba Ya

African Folksong

Childgrove

English Folksong

Eb Alto Saxophone

Blaw the Wind Southerly

English Folksong

Simple Gifts

Shaker Hymn

La Bamba

Spanish Folksong

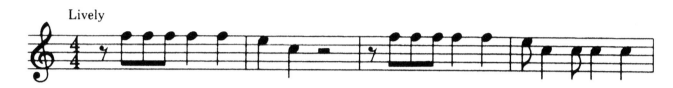

Eb Alto Saxophone

The Ash Grove

English Folksong

Lively

Go Tell Aunt Rhody

American Folksong

Moderate

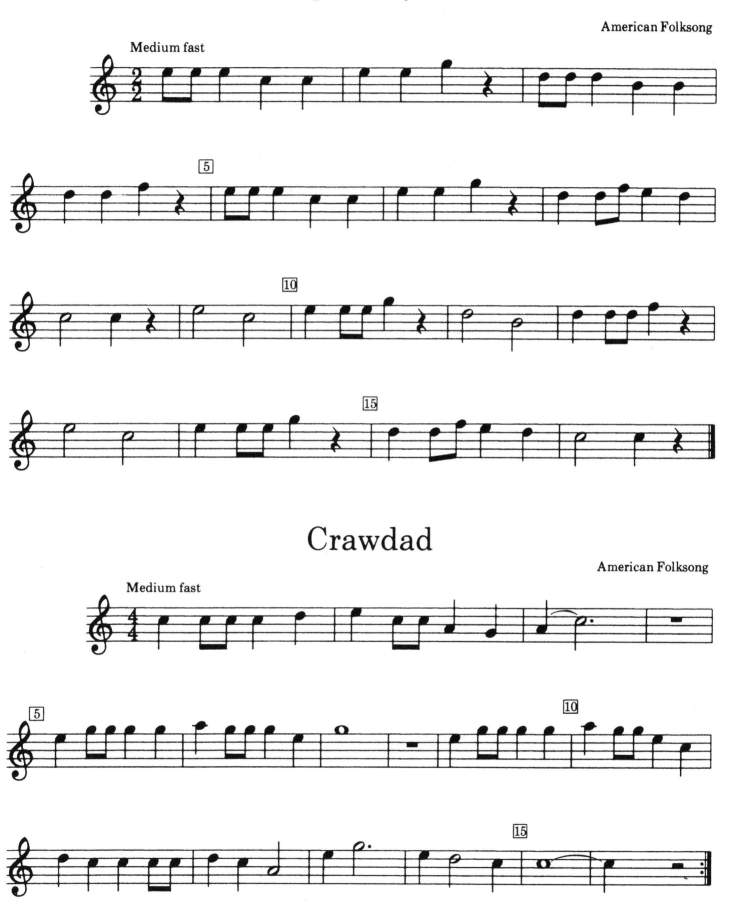

E♭ Alto Saxophone

BLUEGRASS COUNTRY

Old Joe Clarke

Traditional Fiddle Tune

Little Maggie

Fast

Traditional Fiddle Tune

The Rakes of Mallow

Lively

Traditional Fiddle Tune

48144

Eb Alto Saxophone

Will the Circle Be Unbroken

American Folksong

Moderate

Cripple Creek

Traditional Fiddle Tune

16

Eb Alto Saxophone

Arkansas Traveller

Traditional Fiddle Tune

Soldier's Joy

Traditional Fiddle Tune

48144

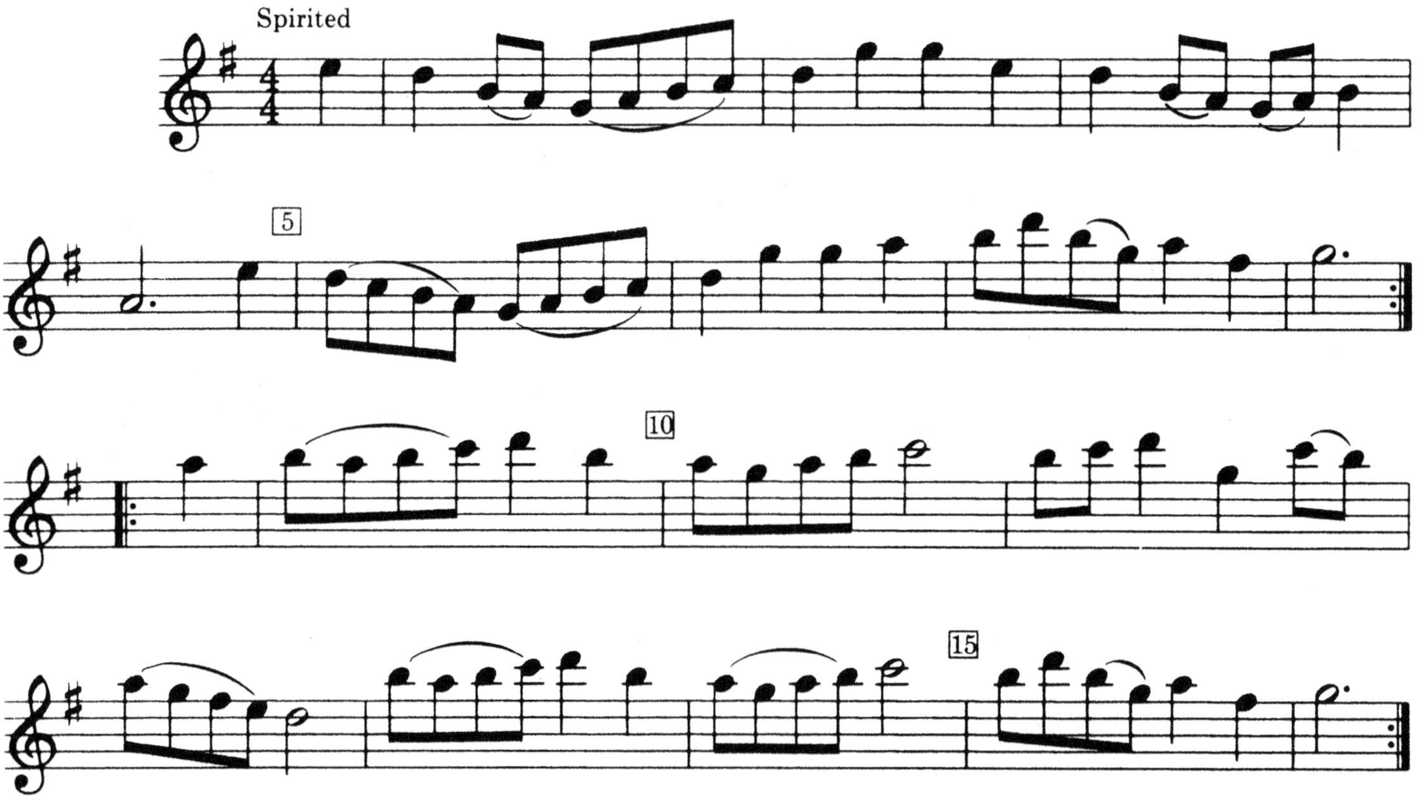

John Henry

American Folksong

Turkey in the Straw

Traditional Fiddle Tune

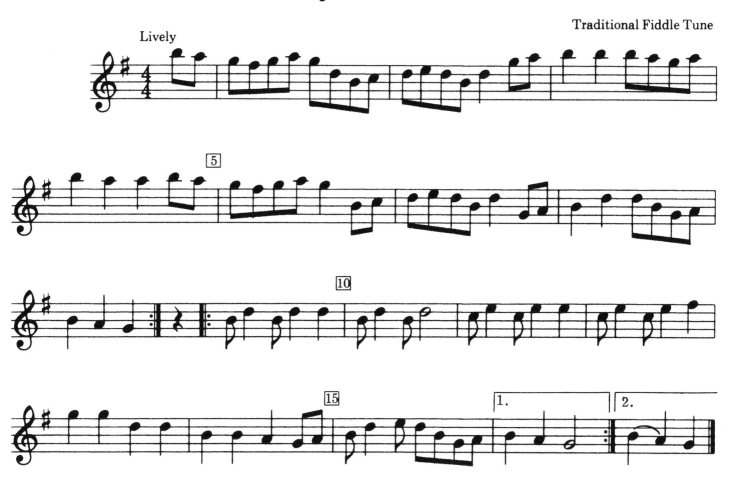

E♭ Alto Saxophone

Worried Man Blues

Traditional Blues

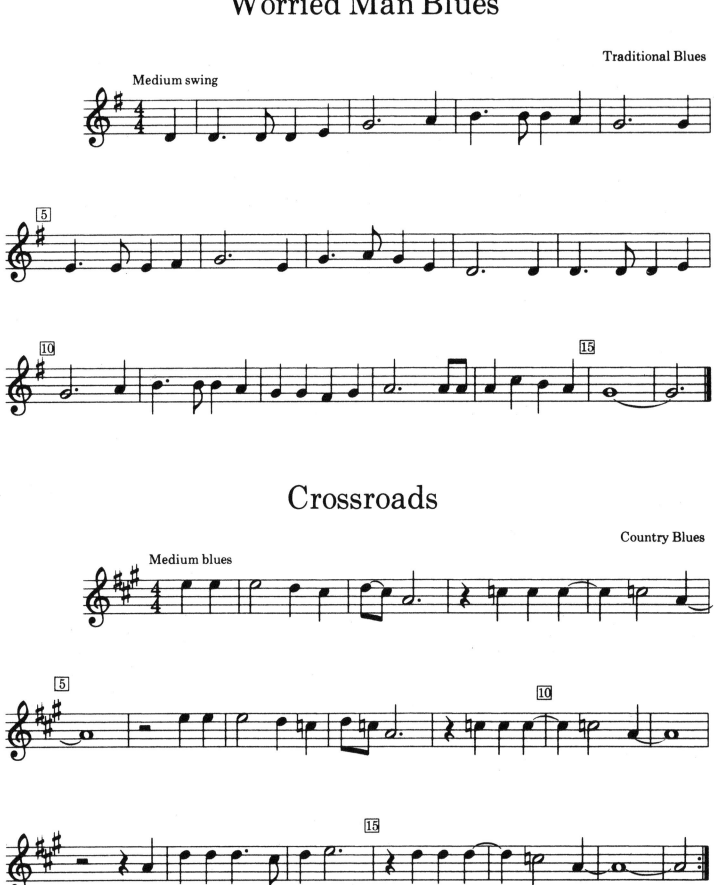

Crossroads

Country Blues

Frankie and Johnny

Relaxed swing

Traditional Blues

Rock My Soul

Lively

Spiritual

Let My People Go

Moderate

Spiritual

Eb Alto Saxophone

Joshua Fought the Battle of Jericho

Spiritual

St. James Infirmary

Traditional Blues

Mama Don't 'low

Folk Blues

Eb Alto Saxophone

Candyman

Country Blues

Camptown Races

Stephen Foster

Eb Alto Saxophone

Shortnin' Bread

Medium swing

Folk Blues

The Entertainer

Moderate

Scott Joplin

Fine

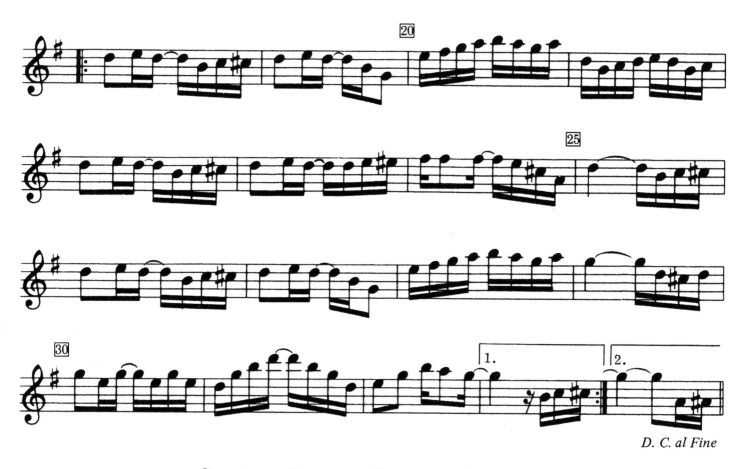

D. C. al Fine

Swing Low, Sweet Chariot

Spiritual

Pistol Blues

Bo'Weevil Jackson

The Chrysanthemum

Scott Joplin